Online Security

Harry Henderson

ReferencePoint
Press®

San Diego, CA

About the Author

Harry Henderson has written more than thirty books on science and technology, particularly computing. He is the author of *The Encyclopedia of Computer Science and Technology*. Henderson lives with his wife, Lisa Yount (a retired writer and active artist), in El Cerrito, California.

For more information, contact:
ReferencePoint Press, Inc.
PO Box 27779
San Diego, CA 92198
www. ReferencePointPress.com

LIBRARY OF CONGRESS CATALOGING-IN-PUBLICATION DATA

Names: Henderson, Harry, 1951- author.
Title: Online security / by Harry Henderson.
Description: San Diego, CA : ReferencePoint Press, Inc., 2017. | Series:
  Digital issues series | Includes bibliographical references and index. |
  Audience: Grade 9 to 12.
Identifiers: LCCN 2016020682 (print) | LCCN 2016022510 (ebook) | ISBN
  9781601529909 (hardback) | ISBN 9781601529916 (eBook)
Subjects: LCSH: Computer security--Juvenile literature. | Computer
  crimes--Prevention--Juvenile literature.
Classification: LCC QA76.9.A25 H45 2017 (print) | LCC QA76.9.A25 (ebook) |
  DDC 005.8--dc23
LC record available at https://lccn.loc.gov/2016020682

CONTENTS

Meeting a Growing Threat

The very power and versatility that makes our digital devices and applications so useful also makes them vulnerable, and often in unexpected ways. In 2009 President Barack Obama made this point when announcing a series of measures designed to protect the nation's computer networks, information systems, and infrastructure. "It's the great irony of our Information Age—the very technologies that empower us to create and to build also empower those who would disrupt and destroy. And this paradox—seen and unseen—is something that we experience every day."[1]

Nearly a decade later, online security continues to be an urgent issue for government, business, and individuals alike. At a 2016 security conference Pierre Nanterme, chief executive officer (CEO) of the management consulting firm Accenture, put the matter in no uncertain terms: "The four biggest challenges the tech industry faces in the coming years are security, security, security and security."[2]

By now, most people have been directly affected by lapses in computer security, or at least know someone who has. Perhaps it was a hijacked e-mail account or a fraudulently used credit card. Some cases can be even more serious: Victims of identity theft can face months of effort to deal with bogus bills and restore good credit.

The stories of individuals struggling in the wake of cybercrime are painful, but they are only the tip of a much larger iceberg. In many cases, behind the stolen credit card, the dubious spam or "phishing" e-mail, or computer virus lies a network of organized crime and an underground economy that deals in stolen information. Indeed, behind the familiar web lies a whole "dark web" whose users' addresses and identities are carefully hidden.

Cybercrime has thus become a lucrative industry that takes in hundreds of millions of dollars a year. In turn, according to a survey by the Ponemon Institute, by 2013, on average, firms with one thousand employees or more were spending about $9 million a year on cybersecurity. Nevertheless, defenses often prove to be inadequate, as customers of some of America's biggest retailers or health insurance companies have found out.

The tools used by hackers to compromise computers, steal information, or shut down websites can be deployed not only by criminals seeking money, but by industrial spies, intelligence agencies (including those of the United States), terrorists, and even activists who seek to expose governments or organizations they think are oppressive. It is believed that billions of dollars' worth of military and trade secrets have been stolen by groups of hackers working in China, Russia, and other countries—but in the shadowy cyberworld, the identity and affiliation of the perpetrators is often unclear, as is what the victims should do in response.

There has also been considerable concern about the twin threats of cyberwar and cyberterrorism. Already, centrifuges used to enrich nuclear fuel in Iran have been destroyed by a computer worm called Stuxnet in an attack meant to slow that country's nuclear weapons program. There have also been attacks on computers and networks in Saudi Arabia, Estonia, and other countries. Planners are now facing the possibility that similar cyberweapons might be used by terrorists or hostile governments to shut down whole power grids, paralyze air traffic, or poison water supplies.

> "The very technologies that empower us to create and to build also empower those who would disrupt and destroy."[1]
>
> —Barack Obama, forty-fourth US president.

Online security is thus a multifaceted problem that does not have a single solution. It is important to develop better technical tools for detecting and blocking attacks. It is also critical to create software, operating systems, and hardware that have better security features. Cooperation—both internationally and between government and business—is needed to address a threat that knows no national boundaries. However, the weakest link

In a 2009 speech at the White House, President Barack Obama announces a series of measures aimed at securing the nation's computer networks, information systems, and infrastructure. The challenge of protecting these vital systems is ongoing.

in many systems is often the human being at the keyboard or on the phone, so people must start seeing themselves as their best defense. That involves becoming more aware of the agendas and techniques used by potential attackers.

Security is vital, but of course it is not the only thing that is important for a thriving, free society. Balances will have to be struck. For example, early in 2016 the need of the FBI to investigate a mass shooting collided with Apple's desire to provide strong encryption for its phones. Similar cases that juggle security with privacy wait in the wings, as do debates over the amount of anonymity people should have online. Anonymity makes criminals hard to catch, but it also protects dissidents and whistle-blowers. Attempts to provide better online security will inevitably raise issues of privacy, consumer rights, corporate accountability, and freedom of expression.

> "The four biggest challenges the tech industry faces in the coming years are security, security, security and security."[2]
>
> —Pierre Nantorme, CEO of the management consulting firm Accenture.

CHAPTER ONE

Threats to Online Security

The online world is no longer a separate realm. Rather, today the whole world is online. As *Wired* magazine editor Ben Hammersley noted in a speech to a British information technology conference: "The Internet is where we live. It's where we do business, where we meet, where we fall in love. . . . There's not much else left. To misunderstand the centrality of these services to today's society is to make a fundamental error. The Internet isn't a luxury addition to life; for most people, knowingly or not, it is life."[3]

Within two decades, the Internet and World Wide Web went from being an interesting research project to an all-encompassing network. Web business was originally led by companies such as Amazon and eBay, but soon mainstream brick-and-mortar stores had to have an online presence if they were to participate in contemporary business. As a result, e-commerce expanded rapidly, bringing billions of dollars' worth of transactions online, along with the associated processing of credit cards. Banks touted the convenience of online account management, while PayPal became a popular way to make payments of all kinds. Next, in the early 2000s, social networks such as Facebook became popular and, for many people and businesses, indispensable. Around the same time, mobile devices such as smartphones became a virtual must-have item, particularly for young people.

All of this money and information have in turn attracted criminals to the online world. Willie Sutton, a prolific American bank robber of the mid-twentieth century, was once asked why he robbed banks. He supposedly replied, "Because that's where the money is."[4] By the late twentieth century, with most money existing in the form of entries in electronic banking and credit card systems, breaking into such systems with a few typed commands was much less risky than using a gun or even a lock pick. There was also less chance of getting caught—traditional bank robbers usually had their careers quickly terminated by the FBI, but law enforcement agencies have often been ill prepared or equipped to cope with cybercrime. Given these factors, threats from online security come from a variety of sources, all of whom share the goal of obtaining valuable information.

> "The Internet isn't a luxury addition to life; for most people, knowingly or not, it is life."[3]
>
> —Ben Hammersley, *Wired* magazine editor.

The Threat from Cybercriminals

Cybercrime pays well. According to cybersecurity expert Jim Lewis, "One pair of cybercriminals made $2 million in one year from click fraud on Facebook. Another pair created those bogus malware warnings that flash on computer screens—the FBI says those cybercriminals made $72 million from people paying to have the phony threats 'removed.'" Cybercrime's lucrative nature is what attracts so many people to it. Says Lewis, "Million-dollar crimes probably happen every month, but are rarely reported."[5]

There are innumerable cybercriminals who seek to profit from other people's data and financial information. A main way such data is stolen is during what is known as a data breach—a massive information grab in which criminals get credit card numbers, names, addresses, Social Security numbers, or health information. In just the past few years, data breaches have involved Home Depot (in which 56 million credit card records were illegally accessed); Staples (in which information from 1.16 million store payment cards was obtained); the medical insurer Anthem (in which 80 million records, including Social Security numbers, were accessed); and the adult dating website Ashley Madison (where hackers obtained personal information about 37 million users).

Besides stealing information in data breaches, cybercriminals also get money from people using extortion, a crime that involves threatening victims with something bad if they refuse to pay. In one extortion scheme, a computer user might be targeted by malware, a secretly loaded program that will open a window that, say, looks like it is from the FBI, the Internal Revenue Service, or even the US Department of Homeland Security. The user may be accused of having illegally downloaded music files, viewing pornography, or perhaps owing taxes or other fees. The user is then threatened with arrest unless he or she pays a "fine." Of course, no legitimate government agency would operate in this way, but fearful victims are often tricked into paying the money.

Sometimes, however, no trickery is needed—just a devastating threat. Cybercriminals may take control of a user's files or content and refuse to give them back until the victim pays. One victim of such a scam was Jim Higgs, the owner of a small AM radio station in Plainwell, Michigan. Since he and his wife are the radio station's only staff, they rely on their PC to provide music and other content. One Friday afternoon, Higgs went down to the basement and heard . . . nothing. Instead of their station playing on the speaker, a pop-up on their computer screen read, "We have locked your files, and you have to pay $500 to get them back."[6] The files containing the music, commercials, and other content needed to run the station had been digitally locked up so they were no longer usable.

> "We have locked your files, and you have to pay $500 to get them back."[6]
>
> —Ransomware message that popped up on victim Jim Higgs's computer.

Higgs and his wife were the victims of ransomware, a new kind of malware that encrypts users' files. The user cannot read or access them, even if the malware can somehow be blocked or bypassed. The user is told to pay up (often hundreds or even thousands of dollars) in order to receive the decryption key and regain file access. Ransomware victims range from small entities

An armed gang robs a bank in the early 1900s. Catching criminals in this era was more straightforward than it is today; the Internet age has greatly complicated law enforcement efforts to track down and prosecute thieves.

like the Higgs to large corporations and organizations. These have included the Hollywood Presbyterian Medical Center in Los Angeles, which in February 2016 was hit with a $3.7 million ransom demand. For a week, vital medical records were inaccessible, and the hospital had to revert to using paper medical records and divert emergency patients to other hospitals. The hospital eventually paid approximately $17,000 in untraceable Internet currency known as Bitcoins to get its medical and billing records back.

The Rise and Fall of the "Silk Road"

As he would write in his journal, Ross Ulbricht had a simple idea: "To create a website where people could buy anything anonymously, with no trail whatsoever that could lead back to them." The marketplace he created was called Silk Road, named for an ancient trade route linking Europe and Asia.

Sellers on the site offered ten thousand products for sale—70 percent were illicit drugs, but one could also buy fake driver's licenses and even some legal products such as pornography that people might not want to purchase openly. To make purchases, buyers used software called Tor to make an anonymous connection and paid with Bitcoins, an encrypted, untraceable currency. According to information gathered by the FBI, from February 2011 to July 2013 Silk Road conducted more than 1.2 million transactions, with about $1.2 billion in sales, earning about $80 million in commissions.

On October 2, 2013, Ulbricht, who operated under the pseudonym "Dread Pirate Roberts," was arrested by the FBI. He was indicted on charges of money laundering, computer hacking, narcotics trafficking, and six attempted murders, although this last charge was later dropped. In February 2015 Ulbricht was found guilty on the other charges and was sentenced to life in prison without parole. Ulbricht's arrest did not put an end to illegal Internet business, of course; following the dismantlement of Silk Road, a Silk Road 2.0 appeared. When that was closed and its alleged owner arrested, it was followed by Silk Road Reloaded.

Quoted in Joshuah Bearman and Tomer Hanuka, "The Rise & Fall of Silk Road, Part 1," *Wired*, April 2015. www.wired.com.

The Threat from Organized Cybercrime and the New Underworld

Online crime has increased because of the scale on which it operates and the resources available to criminals. Online crime is now well organized. Criminal hackers specialize in breaking in to corporate computers containing valuable information such as credit card numbers or in tricking individual users into revealing such information. Other criminals then help turn that stolen information into cash. Stolen credit card numbers are often sold in wholesale lots in online black markets for "carders." Markets for these and many other illicit goods such as drugs and weapons are often part of the dark web. This consists of networks that, while they use the Internet, require special software to access and are thus invisible to ordinary web browsers. On these hidden sites, card numbers are sold in batches to groups of criminals, often in other countries, who use them to buy goods for their own use or to sell to others. That is why someone in Los Angeles whose card has been compromised might suddenly see a credit charge for buying gas in Mexico or expensive electronics goods in Canada.

The revenue from cybercrime allows criminal organizations, particularly in countries such as Russia and other parts of the former Soviet Union, to develop ties with government officials who will turn a blind eye to criminal activity and resist attempts to prosecute it. One example of such a group is the Russian Business Network, which is an Internet service and hosting provider for cybercriminals. Its reasonably priced servers host exchanges that offer the latest exploits (system flaws) discovered by hackers, provide exchanges for carders (to buy and sell stolen credit card numbers), and offer ready-to-use identities and other illegal goods such as weapons, drugs, and child pornography.

Using easy-to-obtain web addresses and readily available hacking tools, organized cybercriminals also use viruses to infect large numbers of personal computers with malware. Using control programs, the infected computers are linked into networks called botnets that in turn can be used to send massive quantities of spam and phishing e-mail or to defraud Internet advertising services by clicking on ads. Alternatively, botnets can be rented out to other criminals for such purposes.

The Threat from Spies

Although most serious attacks on computer systems come from criminals seeking money or valuable information, there can be other motivations to hack into computer networks: to obtain information about technology (such as weapons), military activities, or other developments of interest to intelligence agencies or corporate spies. Since the invention of the telegraph in the mid-nineteenth century, spies around the world have tapped into their enemies' communications in an attempt to gain an advantage with the information gleaned from listening in. Today, however, most communication is carried out through e-mail or other online services, and most companies and governments keep their secrets and other critical information on potentially vulnerable networks. Thus, spies have the opportunity to secretly copy valuable information that belongs to a rival company or country without ever making physical contact.

Plans for the F-35 jet fighter, source code from Google, and details about the Coca-Cola Company's 2009 bid to buy China's Huiyuan Juice Group are among the secrets that have been stolen by such spies. Another target has been the US Office of Personnel Management (OPM), which in June 2015 announced

Spies obtained details of Coca Cola's 2009 bid to buy China's Huiyuan Juice Group. These details were obtained by hacking into online corporate communications and other computer network files.

that it had been the victim of a massive data breach that may have been going on for a year or more. Eventually, the breach was estimated to have compromised as many as 21.5 million records. What is particularly disturbing is that the OPM is the organization that gathers data for security clearances for government employees. Besides personal identification and financial information, such files include details about the person's spouse, parents, close associates, previous addresses, jobs, and schools attended. Jonathan M. Gitlin, a former government policy analyst whose information was obtained, wrote:

"This data isn't mere credit card numbers that can be altered and reissued with minimal pain. It's our lives—histories, relationships, personal appearance, drug use, educational background, and much more."[7]

—Jonathan M. Gitlin, former government policy analyst.

> This data isn't mere credit card numbers that can be altered and reissued with minimal pain. It's our lives—histories, relationships, personal appearance, drug use, educational background, and much more . . . They can't be altered and reissued, and a few months of credit monitoring will do little to protect victims from those determined enough to pull off the heist in the first place.[7]

US officials say they believe the attack originated in China, although China denied any wrongdoing and said that it, too, has been a victim of cyberattacks. It is feared that the information gathered could be used by foreign intelligence agencies to create customized, more believable fake messages that would trick people into revealing even more information about themselves. There could even be opportunities for blackmail. These sobering possibilities have led General Keith Alexander, who served as the head of the National Security Agency (NSA) and then of the US Cyber Command, to describe the loss of American industrial secrets and intellectual property to cyberespionage as "the greatest transfer of wealth in history."[8]

The Other Side of Hacking

Hackers are often portrayed as misguided at best and criminal at worst. In *Hackers: Heroes of the Computer Revolution*, journalist Steven Levy paints a very different picture of hackers. He describes hackers as pioneers who first pushed the boundaries of computing in the 1960s at the Massachusetts Institute of Technology, Stanford, and other universities. Levy describes them as "adventurers, visionaries, risk-takers, [and] artists" who "most clearly saw why the computer was a revolutionary tool." For Levy and many others in computing, this creativity, curiosity, and even obsessive pursuit of new computer applications is what made today's digital world possible. These early hackers created or contributed to the operating systems, programming languages, and other tools software developers use today. This spirit continues today in hackathons, where volunteer programmers and designers come together to work intensively for a few days or weeks to develop new software, often as a public service.

In the field of online security, these good or benevolent hackers are often known as white hats. Unlike black-hat hackers, who have criminal intent, white hats help software makers and companies with large computer networks find and fix vulnerabilities in their system. Some become certified security professionals and engage in systematic "penetration tests," where they try to get into a company's computers using typical hacker tactics—but not to harm anything. Using what they learn, systems can be made more secure and thus resistant to future attacks.

Steven Levy, *Hackers: Heroes of the Computer Revolution*. Sebastapol, CA: O'Reilly, 2010, p. ix.

The Threat from "Hacktivists"

While some people aim to steal information or valuable secrets from governments and businesses, others hack into the computer systems of such entities because of their political or social beliefs.

So-called hacktivists have provided technical support (such as encrypting communications or overriding government censorship protocols) to dissident groups. Hacktivists have also directly targeted governments or institutions with which they disagree. For example, in 2010 the hacktivist group Anonymous attempted to shut down the websites of PayPal and certain credit card companies that had refused to process donations to WikiLeaks, a whistle-blower group that specialized in releasing secret government and corporate documents. Previously, Anonymous had launched attacks against the Church of Scientology (viewed by some opponents as a dangerous cult), while other hacktivists have targeted sites involved with child pornography or human trafficking. No matter their target, hacktivists typically gain access to

Hacktivist groups such as Anonymous (whose symbol is the Guy Fawkes mask, shown here) have launched attacks on governments and institutions to demonstrate disagreement with policies or actions of those entities. In these attacks, hacktivists often gain access to and publicly reveal secret information.

information about their target's activities or even personal details about its employees. The information obtained might be released to the public in order to reveal illegal or objectionable activities (a form of whistle-blowing) or as a form of retaliation.

The best-known hacktivist is Edward Snowden, a government contract employee who had access to top-secret NSA and CIA documents. The documents contained many details of secret global surveillance programs, including one that showed the US government was monitoring civilians' phone calls, e-mails, and other Internet traffic. In 2013, using encrypted e-mail, Snowden leaked the secrets to several newspapers, including the *Guardian* and the *Washington Post*. The US government charged him with espionage and destruction of government property. Snowden then fled US jurisdiction and eventually received political asylum in Russia.

Snowden's actions may have a far-reaching effect on online security. Some of the information he revealed described how intelligence agencies had taken advantage of insecurity in major telecommunications and Internet companies in order to intercept communications. This in turn has led major online companies such as Apple and Google to strengthen their own security (such as through encryption) to protect against government surveillance. Thus, hacktivists like Snowden may both endanger and promote online security.

Threats to online security can arise from many directions and come from people with different motivations or goals. However, whether motivated by greed or ideology, attackers use similar tools and exploit the same sorts of vulnerabilities.

CHAPTER TWO

The Problem with Being Connected

Online attacks can happen to anyone, and they can happen very quickly. Writing in *Wired* magazine in 2012, Mat Honan recounts, "In the space of one hour, my entire digital life was destroyed. First my Google account was taken over, then deleted. Next my Twitter account was compromised, and used as a platform to broadcast racist and homophobic messages. And worst of all, my AppleID account was broken into, and my hackers used it to remotely erase all of the data on my iPhone, iPad, and MacBook."[9]

But how is it possible for criminals to break in to computer systems, steal information, or trick users into revealing credit card numbers or passwords? It turns out that the very things that make computers such powerful tools also make them vulnerable to being misused.

What Makes Computers Vulnerable?

Computers have taken many routine tasks out of humans' hands, performing them quickly, efficiently, and for the most part, reliably. When connected to networks, computer programs can draw on many sources of information to provide their services. The combination of speed, capacity, and connectivity is how billions of transactions can be processed each day, from corporate payrolls to eBay auctions to summoning rides using the popular transportation app

Uber. However, these same qualities of automation, speed, and connectivity also allow hackers to bombard millions of users with spam and scam messages at virtually no cost, or enable attackers to probe thousands of machines looking for flaws. The ease of connectivity means that once a way into a computer is found, an attacker can quickly probe other connected devices to obtain more information.

Another thing computers do really well is make copies of things and spread them around, whether they be cat videos on YouTube, pirated movie downloads on sketchy websites, or millions of tweets and retweets that go out each day on Twitter. However, any computer program itself is, at its core, just another string of 1s and 0s that stand for numbers or letters, the same as any other kind of data. That means programs can also copy themselves, and the new copy can do all the things the original could do. That is essentially the logic behind a computer virus.

Early computer viruses could only spread if a person physically moved floppy disks from one computer to another, like a disease that only spreads by direct contact. However, when the use of online services grew in the 1980s, allowing users to share and download software, viruses became able to spread somewhat more rapidly. Then the growing use of the Internet and the World Wide Web in the early 1990s created a computer virus epidemic, which presented wide-ranging threats to online security. Viruses could now spread like the flu through the "air" of cyberspace.

The Internet: Reliable yet Vulnerable

The Internet was not designed with security in mind. Its objective was to enable computers to connect to one another reliably and automatically. After all, it would have been hard to anticipate in the 1970s or even 1980s that computer networks would be so directly involved with everyday business, corporate and government operations, and even warfare.

The basic idea of the Internet is simple but powerful. By having an agreed-upon format for addressing and routing information packets, the network allows any kind of device that understands that format to communicate with anyone or anything else in the world—a laptop or desktop computer, a phone, even a car. For example, a web browser can request a page from a website's server using a protocol (set of rules) called HTTP. To do so, the browser connects to a router in the user's home or office, which controls access from the local computer (or network) to the Internet. (Alternatively, with a mobile device, the connection is made

An Uber user summons a ride. Speed, capacity, and connectivity make it possible for the popular transportation app and many other companies to process billions of transactions each day.

over the cellular network to the phone provider's routers.) The web request then makes its way to the website through a series of routers that keep constantly updated lists of addresses showing available connections, using something called Domain Name System, or DNS.

Because of its flexibility, the routing system is remarkably reliable. If a server goes down, data can still get to its destination through an alternate route. However, there are various ways in which hackers can subvert the system for their own purposes. For example, they might insert their own routing information, in effect hijacking the web traffic and sending it to a server that they control. They might also have their server masquerade as the legitimate server, which also allows them to intercept the traffic. To do such things, attackers generally use vulnerabilities in either the software that runs web servers or the software that is responsible for the addressing and routing system.

Malware and Botnets

With so many people connected and so much valuable information online, it is no wonder that criminals would find ways to use malicious software, also known as malware. Malware includes worms, viruses, Trojans, and other kinds of programs that can be placed on a user's computer to carry out a variety of criminal schemes or even take over control of the computer itself.

Contemporary ways of accessing content and information have further enabled such crime. Today, for example, people generally do not get their software, music, and other media from disks but directly from websites and online services. A modern web server uses many components to present this content to a user. These components add many useful capabilities, but each represents a potential weak link. By taking advantage of any one of these weaknesses, an attacker can insert or modify program code on the server. As a result, when a user clicks on a link, malware can be downloaded and secretly installed on the user's computer.

There are many types of malware. The less harmful types might just show annoying ads. More commonly, malware such

Anatomy of a Data Breach

In late 2013 a well-organized group of hackers operating in Russia pulled off one of the biggest cyber-robberies in history. First they found a weak point in the networks of the Target Corporation, one of the world's largest retailers. They then inserted malware that installed itself in the company's thousands of cash registers. When a customer swiped a credit or debit card, the card's data was routed to one of three Target servers that had been hijacked. A few days later, the collected data began to be sent to the hackers' servers in Russia.

This activity triggered an alarm set up via FireEye, Target's sophisticated $1.6 million antimalware system. However, for reasons that were never made clear, Target officials did not respond to the alert. As a result, the criminals successfully retrieved the card data and presumably sold it on the underground criminal market.

In the first three months after the attack, Target spent $61 million dealing with the breach, which included paying for affected customers to have their credit monitored for fraud. Later, Target paid about $40 million more in reparations to credit card companies and banks. They also spent about $100 million for new cash registers that worked with newer, more secure chip cards that are beginning to replace the older, more vulnerable magnetic strip cards. Including the estimated loss in sales and profits because of customers deciding not to shop there during the holiday season due to security concerns, in all the breach cost Target about $300 million.

as keyloggers can intercept information (such as a password) that is entered by the user and send it to a computer designated by the malware. The most pernicious form of malware takes control of the target computer so it will execute any instructions that are sent to it. By controlling and coordinating thousands of such computers, the attacker creates a botnet. The computers that make up botnets can in turn be used to send out millions of spam messages, run an illicit server to sell illegal products (such as drugs), or conduct fraud.

Another way to leverage the power of a botnet is to have its computers send out simultaneous page requests to a targeted web server. Such a distributed denial of service attack, or DDoS, can make a website unresponsive to legitimate users. Because many businesses operate solely online and most need their websites to run around the clock, a DDoS can lead to lost business. A DDoS can also be the basis of a protection racket: A company might be threatened with an attack unless it pays for protection, for example. However, DDoS can also be used by dissident groups to protest government actions or by repressive governments to silence dissidents.

If the target is lucrative enough (perhaps a big bank or a defense contractor involved with advanced weapons), a large, coordinated effort called an advanced persistent threat might be made to obtain the desired information. Attackers may scout the organization for weeks or months, looking for systems that might be vulnerable and gathering personal details about key persons. The actual attack might involve sending out fake e-mails to trick these people into downloading malware that in turn will ferret out their passwords or other secure information. Once the accounts are accessed, information from databases can be copied, as quietly as possible to try to delay discovery of the attack.

Spammed and Scammed

While criminals can steal large quantities of information directly from servers, they can also trick individual users into revealing personal information or installing malware on their computers. Hackers call such techniques social engineering. The most common form of social engineering is called phishing, which uses "bait" to try to get the e-mail recipient to respond.

In a typical example of phishing, many thousands of spam e-mails may be sent. They may claim to be, say, from a major bank. The messages will use logos, language, and other features that are similar to those used by the bank, and the e-mail address from which they are sent can be altered to appear similar to the real one. The message might include realistic-sounding text, such as the following:

Dear Valued Customer,

For your security, Wells Fargo bank has safeguard your account. . . . You now need to verify your identity.

To verify your identity, kindly follow reference below and take the directions to instant activation.[10]

An observant user might notice that the message doesn't re-fer to the account holder specifically, as would be the case in a legitimate notice. The grammatical errors also suggest that the message was written by someone who is not very familiar with the English language, which could also indicate it originates from spam producers in countries such as Nigeria or Russia. However, as phishing messages become increasingly sophisticated, one cannot always count on such clues.

Phishing e-mails always include a link to a website, but the site it connects the victim to is a carefully designed replica of the real site. If the user enters the requested infor-mation, it is intercepted by the hacker and can then be used to access the real account and drain it of money.

An important aspect of phishing mes-sages is that they are designed to create an emotional "rush" that overrides normal caution. They often feature content that is steeped in fear ("You're going to lose access to your account"), greed ("You've won a prize!"), or even compas-sion ("Your grandson has been in an accident abroad and needs money"). Phishing messages can target individuals or large cor-porations. For example, more than 200 million records of Target

> "To verify your identity, kindly follow reference below and take the directions to instant activation."[10]
>
> —Phishing message claiming to come from a bank.

Home Depot (pictured) and Target are among large corporations that have been hit by phishing scams. When customer data is stolen through such scams, companies often experience huge financial losses.

and Home Depot customers were stolen in 2013 and 2014 when administrator accounts were obtained through phishing. The financial losses in such cases are staggering; in 2014, for example, Microsoft estimated that the worldwide impact of phishing could be as much as $5 billion.

Social Media: New Opportunities for Attack

Much of the activity carried out by malware and botnets aims to obtain personal information that can be used for credit card or identity fraud. Often, however, criminals do not even need to hack into a system to find such information. In many cases, people have already provided it via their use of social networks such as Facebook.

Many social network users underestimate the amount of sensitive information they make available about themselves. For example, suppose someone posts on Facebook that he or she is excited to leave next Monday for a three-week vacation in Europe. Someone who checks for such postings on behalf of a local burglary ring might be interested to know that a house is likely to become vacant. Moreover, it is easy to find someone's address with a few targeted online searches or by using a lookup service.

Consider another bit of information freely shared on many social media sites: a person's date of birth. Birthdays are often used to verify identity for medical or other records, and they are very helpful for anyone seeking to create a profile that brings together information about a specific person. Now, suppose someone puts up a Facebook time line post dated April 11, 2016, and writes, "Today's my 30th birthday!" Anyone who knows how to subtract can now deduce that person's date of birth.

There is thus enough information online—either collected in the course of business or voluntarily posted on social networking sites—for criminals to steal others' identity or trick them with a carefully designed phishing message. In this way, information that is online is like a jigsaw puzzle; while the individual pieces of information might seem unimportant, when they come together, a rich and valuable picture emerges.

However, people are becoming more aware of the risks of divulging sensitive information. According to the online certification service TRUSTe, in 2016, 45 percent of respondents were more worried about their online privacy than they were the previous year. When asked why, 36 percent cited security as a top concern, and 74 percent said they were actually limiting their online activity due to privacy concerns. This included not clicking on an ad, not downloading an app (or stopping the use of an app), or avoiding certain websites.

Unhealthy Exposure: Stolen Medical Records and Identity Theft

The health industry is another area of life that has gone online—both to patients' advantage and detriment. For example, electronic medical records contain detailed information about test results, procedures, medications, and diagnoses. As such, they offer health professionals the ability to monitor their patients' ongoing care more efficiently and prevent dangerous errors. However, when digitized, medical records are vulnerable to hacking—which is troubling, given the fact that they are rich sources of sensitive personal information.

Medical records contain intimate information, such as whether a patient has conditions such as HIV/AIDS or cancer, has a history of substance abuse or mental illness, or takes certain medications that compromise the ability to do certain tasks. Such people could be subject to discrimination if an employer (or prospective employer) obtained this information. They could even be blackmailed with the threat of revealing such sensitive information.

However, the bigger risk for most people is found in the non-medical part of the record—information such as their Social Security number, address, and date of birth. This data can be used to steal a victim's identity, enabling criminals to open credit accounts in the victim's name and run up thousands of dollars in debt. Unlike a credit card, which can be quickly canceled, a person's name and personal details are essentially permanent and could be used even many years later. According to the Ponemon Institute, a privacy research group, identity theft stemming from medical records doubled between 2010 and 2015.

The consequences for victims of medical identity theft can be serious and long lasting. The Ponemon Institute estimates that the average victim will spend $13,500 and two hundred hours of time trying to deal with the bogus accounts opened by identity thieves and attempting to repair his or her credit. This is similar to the consequences of any identity theft. What is potentially worse is that the thieves often try to use the medical record to obtain prescription drugs or medical equipment. This can end up introducing incorrect information into the record, which in turn could lead to later errors in the real patient's diagnosis or treatment.

Because of the value of the information contained in medical records and the potential to abuse products and services, some of the biggest data breaches in recent years have occurred in the health care field. Federal law requires that breaches be reported, and in 2015 the government tallied 253 health care insurers or health care

A doctor talks with her patient about a medical condition. Many doctor's offices and hospitals rely on electronic medical records, which make it easier and more efficient to monitor a patient's ongoing care but are also vulnerable to damaging data breaches.

systems that had been breached, involving a total of 112 million records. A single breach of records held by the insurance company Anthem, for example, involved 78.8 million individuals.

Mobile Devices: Always On, Always Vulnerable

During many online activities, someone might connect to a site or service, post a message or buy a product, and then end the connection. However, with the rapidly growing use of smartphones, tablets, and wearable devices, many people are connected virtually all the time. This constant connection means there are many more opportunities for phishing, introducing malware, or performing some other sort of attack.

Another thing that adds to the vulnerability of mobile devices is the way their software is developed and the features included in

Hacking the Vote?

Public confidence in the fairness of elections is vital for any democracy. However, democracy itself is threatened by cybercrime when the machines used to record votes in elections can be tampered with. This was proved possible in 2008, when two university students got hold of an AVC Edge electronic voting machine. To graphically demonstrate its vulnerability, the students reprogrammed it to play the 1980s hit video game *Pac-Man*. Crucially, they did so without breaking the seals that were supposed to let officials know that the machines had not been tampered with.

In recent years, many polling places have moved to some form of electronic voting. This worries many security experts, who warn it is possible to tamper with the recording or tabulating of digitally cast votes. In 2012 researcher Roger Johnston demonstrated how two machines—the Diebold Accuvote-TSX and the Sequoia AVC—could be hacked. Johnston inserted a tiny chip that would change a vote cast for a candidate named Smith to one that was recorded as a vote cast for a candidate named Jones. "We can do this because most voting machines, as far as I can tell, are not encrypted," warned Johnston. "It's just open standard format communication. Anyone who does digital electronics—a hobbyist or an electronics fan—could figure this out." Such an attack requires physical access to the machine, but voting machines are typically stored for months with minimal security. Indeed, this underscores a critical point regarding online security: Sometimes the weakest link in cybersecurity is actually the lack of adequate physical security.

Quoted in Roger Johnston, "How I Hacked an Electronic Voting Machine," *Popular Science*, November 5, 2012. www.popsci.com.

these devices. With mobile devices, app developers can draw on many new sources of online information, such as maps, data about businesses, and links to social networking sites. Meanwhile, mobile devices now include many ways to obtain information about the user's environment, including cameras, microphones, Global Positioning System (GPS) locators, motion and acceleration sensors, and more. Many apps are necessarily "location aware" and track users in order to connect them to services, whether it be potential dates, rides, shopping, or dining opportunities. However, this means that information about a person's whereabouts and daily activities is potentially available to hackers. In general, data on mobile devices is often poorly protected.

Thus, attackers ofton have an easy way in to devices—through the apps that run on them. Many apps are not designed with security in mind, and in their rush to get them to market, many developers engage in little or no security testing. A recent study by the Ponemon Institute found that about one-third of the companies surveyed did not test their apps for security at all.

Taking further advantage of poor security, attackers can make fake versions of popular apps and offer them to unsuspecting users for download. (While some companies such as Apple carefully screen apps before they are offered on their app store, users of so-called jailbroken devices that bypass restrictions can download apps directly from any website.)

Not just individual users but whole organizations can be severely impacted by poor mobile security. Many people want to use their personal phones, tablets, and other devices at work. After all, they are familiar with them, and the devices include their favorite apps. However, if a device has been infected by malware (perhaps via a software flaw or bogus app), that device can be used by a remote intruder to steal information from the company when the employee uses it to access its network.

With so many kinds of devices, apps, and services, securing the online world has thus become a daunting task. Threats seem to come from every direction, and the techniques used to steal information are constantly evolving and becoming more sophisticated.

CHAPTER THREE

Building a Safer Cyberspace

At McAfee, one of the leading computer security firms, researchers find a new species of malware every second. Their ongoing collection of such specimens numbered more than 110 million by 2013. Besides antivirus and security firms, other major Internet-based companies such as Amazon, Google, Apple, Microsoft, Facebook, and Twitter deploy their own resources to try to keep their users safe. According to the Gartner research group, annual spending by organizations and individuals worldwide on security software is projected to reach $101 billion by 2018. This indicates the extent of the problem of computer security and the kinds of resources being spent trying to solve it.

Despite all these efforts, when asked about the future, experts worry that the problem is likely to get worse, not better. A majority of participants in interviews and workshops at the World Economic Forum, for example, believed that attackers would have an increasing edge over defenders, with attacks becoming more sophisticated and coming faster than defenses can keep up with. As one participant, a pharmaceutical executive, noted, "[The attackers only] need to get lucky once and have the ability to evolve so rapidly. . . . Our large company just isn't agile enough to match [their] pace."[11]

Defense in Depth: Securing Websites and Apps

Each organization that has a network or website is ultimately responsible for its own security. But what does it mean to say that a system has good security? Security is often viewed as a triangle built from three components: confidentiality, integrity, and availability. Confidentiality means the ability to keep data (whether payroll information, medical records, or engineering plans for a new smartphone) restricted only to those persons who should have access to it. Integrity means ensuring that data has not been tampered with—deleted or even subtly altered, as young hackers have sometimes done with school grades. Availability means that the system is up and running when needed. A secure system is one that has all three of these features working simultaneously. If, for example, a system has good data integrity and backups but no procedures to quickly recover from an incident, that is not good enough from a business point of view. After all, a beautifully designed, fully functional website is of no use if it is not online.

Administrators have tools to ensure that their systems achieve confidentiality, integrity, and availability. One is to run a system that features access permissions. These allow employees to see only the information they need to do their jobs; such a system is more likely to preserve confidentiality. This way, if a hacker tricks a low-level employee into giving up his or her password, the hacker would be able to obtain only limited information. Still, some of that information might include the names of higher-level superiors, who might then become susceptible to attacks themselves. To preserve integrity, regular audits can check databases, perhaps comparing their contents to records stored in backups in order to find differences that might indicate tampering or data corruption. Backups are also crucial for restoring availability if, for example, a

> [The attackers only] need to get lucky once and have the ability to evolve so rapidly. . . . Our large company just isn't agile enough to match [their] pace."[11]
>
> —A drug company executive at the World Economic Forum.

website has been defaced or a PC user's hard drive data has been locked up in a ransomware attack.

Security Tools

Of course, the goal of security is to prevent attacks from succeeding in the first place, and that is where a variety of other tools, such as antivirus programs, come into play. Most computer users are aware of the need to run an antivirus program on their machine. Generally, such a program checks files on the hard drive (and files incoming from e-mail attachments or the web) against a constantly updated list of signatures, or patterns of bits of program code of known viruses. Many operating systems such as Microsoft Windows include basic antivirus, antimalware, and firewall programs, and more advanced products can also be purchased.

Unfortunately, antivirus and antimalware programs are like flu shots: They are a very good idea, but you still may get the flu. That is because like the flu, malware comes in many different strains and is constantly evolving. A 2014 study by Lastline Labs found that most newly discovered malware was undetected by most existing antivirus programs. Even after two months of a virus circulating over the Internet, about a third of the programs failed to detect it.

The most dangerous situation occurs when someone finds a previously unknown flaw—called a zero day exploit—in an operating system's program code, web browser, or other widely used program. Malware that takes advantage of such a flaw is less likely to be detected by antivirus programs, because the code exploiting it does not match any known pattern. Thus, knowledge of such flaws is a prized commodity on the criminal black market. Indeed, security expert Brian Krebs notes that "on any given day, nation-states and criminal hackers have access to an entire arsenal of zero-day vulnerabilities."[12] Details of zero-day vulnerabilities are actually being stockpiled both by governments

> "On any given day, nation-states and criminal hackers have access to an entire arsenal of zero-day vulnerabilities."[12]
>
> —Security expert Brian Krebs.

and hacker groups, rather than being used immediately to attack systems. That way, they can be saved up in order to possibly penetrate a system in the future.

While antivirus programs focus on detecting and neutralizing malware in a computer system, another line of defense attempts to stop intruders before they can even enter. If someone wants to avoid getting a physical infection, it is a good idea to eat well and get lots of rest (to keep the immune system healthy) and be careful about cuts that might get infected. In the digital world, the "skin" that tries to keep infection out is called a firewall. Firewalls are programs that watch communications between a computer and the Internet. They are built into routers and most operating systems, so the average user who connects to the Internet is often protected by two firewalls.

A firewall uses a programmable set of rules to determine which data packets will be accepted and forwarded to the computer.

For example, if a stream of packets from an unexpected Internet address is coming in, it may indicate an intruder is probing the system, checking for potential vulnerabilities. If so, the firewall will reject the packets. There are also many standard connections, or ports, for services such as HTTP (web), FTP (file transfer), or SMTP (e-mail). The firewall can be configured to have certain ports open while shutting others that are not needed for normal operations and could be vulnerable (to uploading files containing viruses, for example). Since hackers often run automated programs that scan the network for open, vulnerable ports, a properly configured firewall will cause most hackers to look elsewhere, just as a good deadbolt on a door or a sticker from an alarm company may encourage a burglar to move on to a different house. More sophisticated firewalls can also use information about typical and problematic traffic to identify and block attacks.

Beyond Passwords

In addition to exploiting software flaws, intruders also seek to log in to user accounts that might contain valuable information or provide greater access to a system. The most basic protection against such unauthorized access is passwords. Just about the most common advice given to computer users is to use strong, hard-to-guess passwords for important accounts such as those pertaining to e-mail, banking, or shopping. Virtually any password can be cracked given enough time—but time is money even for criminals, and there is no reason to make things easier for them.

Still, passwords provide only basic security. Not only can they be guessed, they can also be obtained by breaking in to the servers that store them. Just as a medieval castle that had a moat and a wall was more secure than one that only had a wall, a computer log-in process can be more secure if it poses multiple hurdles to a would-be intruder. A good rule of thumb in security is to require users to provide something they know, something they have, or something they are. The something they know can be a traditional password. To get money out of an ATM, however, one needs both the password, in the form of a personal identification number, or PIN ("something they know") and the physical card ("something they have"). The digital equivalent of this is to require that a person also has something physical. Most commonly, if someone is logging in from a different computer, the system might send a code to the user's phone, which would then be typed in to complete the log-in.

A final security precaution is to have users provide information related to "something they are"—that is, something that pertains to their unique physical identity, such as their fingerprints, the pattern of tiny blood vessels in their eye, or their facial geometry. Such details are known as biometrics, and systems that require them for access—which increasingly include smartphones and laptops—can eliminate the hassle and potential vulnerability of using passwords. Still, biometric devices and systems themselves may have poor security and could be fooled or tampered with.

A biometric scanner that identifies a person through the blood vessels in the hand is used to grant or deny entry at a data processing center in Germany. Biometric scanners may prove to be a more secure option than passwords.

Bug Bounties Harness Hackers for Good

Many of the biggest private companies on the Internet (such as Google, Facebook, Yahoo!, and Microsoft) offer bug bounties—rewards for finding and reporting flaws in their own software or in other software used by program developers. In 2013 even the Pentagon adopted this strategy. Defense Digital Service director Christopher Lynch invited hackers to help the government find flaws in defense department systems. "If you have the skills and care about making America more secure, I hope you'll sign up and give it a shot," he said. "Bringing in the best practices from [the] private sector will help us truly transform the federal government, and I'd like you to come along with us."

However, while anyone can report a bug, in order to be paid for their work, participants must pass a basic criminal background screening and meet other conditions. The problem is that many of the most talented hackers are likely to have fallen afoul of the criminal justice system at one time or another. Nevertheless, government and private bug bounties have proved to be an effective way to strengthen software while channeling hacking skills in a more positive direction.

Quoted in Sean Sposito, "Some Skeptical of Defense Department's Hack the Pentagon Pilot," *San Francisco Chronicle*, April 11, 2016. www.sfchronicle.com.

Fighting the Phishers

Even with the best security, criminals will find ways to reach people online. E-mail filters included in services such as Google's Gmail have become increasingly good at blocking spam and messages suspected of containing phishing messages. Nevertheless, what makes spam a viable business model is that, assuming one has access to an e-mail server (perhaps on a hijacked computer), sending a million e-mail messages costs no more than sending one. Thus, even if only a tiny percentage of recipients responds to a spam mailing, considerable profits are possible. It is no wonder that as of 2015 a bit over half of all e-mail sent is spam. Even with good filters in place, some spam messages will get through. Moreover, other forms of communication such as text messaging, messaging apps such as WhatsApp, and postings on social networks are much less well guarded than e-mail and thus increasingly used by spammers.

Phishing messages can harm individuals by getting them to give up money or personal financial information. From a security point of view, however, the threat from phishing is that it can enable attackers to learn what information they need to penetrate further into the system, often using the privileged accounts of executives or administrators. The following example illustrates how a sophisticated attack that used this kind of approach managed to get into RSA, one of the world's top cybersecurity companies. First the attacker sent phishing e-mails with the subject line "2011 Recruitment Plan" to a small number of employees. The company's phishing filter moved the messages to the "Junk" folder. Unfortunately, since one can get false positives (messages marked as spam that actually are not such), one employee saw the message, thought it was legitimate, and opened it.

The message contained an Excel spreadsheet as an attachment. When the employee clicked on it, the spreadsheet (which is actually a sort of program in itself) ran malware. The malware took advantage of a previously undisclosed zero-day flaw in Adobe's Flash animation software. This enabled the malware to install a back door that allowed outside hackers to install further software on the machine. The hacker took control of the machine and obtained several of the users' passwords that provided access to sensitive data, which was sent to another hacked machine, and finally back to the hacker. RSA said that the attack could weaken the effectiveness of its SecurID software, which many companies rely on to authenticate users who log on to their systems.

Some might say that the fact that the hack was eventually discovered means the security was actually rather good. But the human error that made the hack possible shows just how hard it is to prevent attackers from finding the one weak link they need to strike. Therefore, training users to recognize phishing and other forms of social engineering, along with using a combination of filters and tools, offers the best chance of preventing potentially devastating data breaches.

Protecting Data with Encryption

If intruders cannot actually read the information they obtain, it is not of any use to them. Therefore, encryption is one of the most important lines of defense for protecting crucial information. Encryption uses mathematical formulas and algorithms that turn ordinary, readable text into gibberish that can only be decoded by someone who has the proper key. (In a browser, a web address that includes a padlock symbol and an "https:" address indicates that encryption is being used to protect data that is sent to that site.)

Unfortunately, the most commonly used encryption system— called public key cryptography—is not foolproof. The system is set up so that each person who wants to communicate has a public key and a private key. To send someone a message, the sender encrypts it with the recipient's public key. The message can only be decrypted using the recipient's private key. As long as the private key is kept private, the communication is secure.

The problem lies in the need to verify that the public key actually belongs to the designated company or person. When accessing the site, the browser uses security software to verify that the site has a valid digital certificate (a sort of digital signature) by comparing it with that stored by an organization called a certificate authority. However, an intruder who can steal a public key (or perhaps tamper with the certificate authority) can intercept and decode financial transactions or other critical information involving sites that use that certification.

Resilience and Recovery

Despite the best efforts, security will be breached, and thus the security industry has promoted the concept of resilience. Resilience is a combination of preparedness, flexibility, and resourcefulness.

A team from Switzerland takes part in a cybersecurity competition as part of a 2015 international conference on cyberattacks and defense. Cybersecurity experts are continually testing systems from inside and out to enhance their ability to detect and respond to attacks.

In computer security, resilience is the ability of an organization and its online systems to anticipate, prepare for, and respond to attacks effectively.

Being prepared means that rather than waiting for something to go wrong, security experts constantly probe the system from outside (playing the role of the hacker) in order to find weaknesses, hopefully before they are discovered by criminals. Such testing should also include phishing and other social engineering attempts. Knowing such tests may occur at any time will keep personnel on their toes and ready to spot something that does not seem right. In their book on cybersecurity, authors P.W. Singer and Allan Friedman describe other aspects of resilience, including realizing that defenses will fail sometimes and that one

Careers in Information Security

With the ever increasing number of cyberattacks, it is no wonder that information security specialists are in high demand. According to the Bureau of Labor Statistics, employment in information security is expected to grow 18 percent from 2014 to 2024, making it one of the fastest-growing occupations.

What qualities are important in a person who wants to become a security specialist? Both big-picture intuition and attention to detail are required. Intuition allows one to sense when something in a database or network is not as it should be or that a user's behavior is not typical. However, much of the work of maintaining computer security requires managing the day-to-day details—systematically running tests, reading data logs and incident reports, evaluating new security tools, and making sure each piece of software in the system is kept up-to-date with the latest security "fixes."

How might one prepare for a career in this field? College courses (including online courses) in computer science and programming can provide a good general background. (Some colleges offer degrees or specializations in computer security.) Actual experience as a network or system administrator or a developer or tester of software is also important. This is how one becomes familiar with the environment in which security analysts work and the kinds of problems they face. One way to get some of this experience is to volunteer to help a school or nonprofit organization set up and maintain its computer system, website, or network.

should learn how to respond appropriately. The authors compare this kind of resilience to how the human body responds to injury or infection:

> Your body still figures out a way to continue functioning even if your external layer of defense—your skin—is penetrated by a cut or even bypassed by an attack like a viral

infection. Just as in the body, in the event of a cyber incident, the objective should be to prioritize resources and operations, protect key assets and systems from attacks, and ultimately restore normal operations.[13]

Damage can be minimized by detecting and responding to an attack as quickly as possible. Affected machines or databases can be isolated from the rest of the system to limit the spread of malware. The extent of the attack and its effects can then be determined. It is essential that data be backed up regularly so the system can be restored after an attack or other disaster.

Another way to practice resilience is to realize that not just systems but human relationships may need to be "repaired" following an attack. Consider that organizations often neglect to communicate with affected customers about a breach when it happens. Customers need to know that the company understands how important security is to them, and they need to know what measures are being taken to protect their data better. After all, if a major breach causes people to lose confidence in the security of their data, the loss of future business might be even more costly than the attack itself.

> "In the event of a cyber incident, the objective should be to prioritize resources and operations, protect key assets and systems from attacks, and ultimately restore normal operations."[13]
>
> —Security analysts P.W. Singer and Allan Friedman.

CHAPTER FOUR

Regulating and Policing the Digital Realm

The developers and entrepreneurs who have largely been responsible for creating the modern online world often seem to want to minimize government regulation. Some think that regulators do not understand enough about how the technology works and what it needs to flourish. For example, Eric Schmidt, executive chair of Alphabet (and before that, Google) notes, "The Internet is the first thing that humanity has built that humanity doesn't understand, the largest experiment in anarchy that we have ever had."[14] Similarly, back in the 1990s cyberlibertarian activist John Perry Barlow suggested that the online world could regulate itself. "Where there are real conflicts, where there are wrongs, we will identify them and address them by our means," said Barlow. "We are forming our own Social Contract. This governance will arise according to the conditions of our world, not yours. Our world is different."[15]

Self-policing and lack of government intervention may have been sufficient when the Internet essentially belonged to a few thousand computer scientists and researchers, but it is clearly not adequate when scaled up to a web that several billion people use to engage in transactions that involve trillions of dollars, and where breakdowns—from attacks or otherwise—could cause major economic disruptions or even disasters such as widespread power failures. The question then becomes not whether the government should have a role in securing cyberspace, but what that role should be, and how government and private organizations might best work together.

Law Enforcement and Cybercrime

The government has two basic roles in dealing with cybercrime: enforcing laws and developing policy (including legislation and regulation). Both of these areas raise numerous challenges. One of the biggest challenges for law enforcement is to become aware that an attack has happened in the first place. Suppose a major organization such as a retailer, bank, or insurance company suffers a data breach. Although sometimes an attack can be detected while it is in progress, in many cases it is only discovered weeks or months after it happens. (In 2015 research by the Ponemon Institute and IBM found that it takes an average of 256 days to detect a cyberattack.) Imagine if a bank discovered that its vault had been emptied by robbers only after more than half a year had passed!

Once investigators from agencies such as the FBI do become aware of a data theft or other cyberattack, they face further challenges. Unlike traditional crimes, where fingerprints or other physical evidence can help investigators quickly narrow the list of possible suspects, in cybercrime the evidence is bits of data that may or may not mean anything. In some cases the data might be e-mail or web addresses that may appear to come from a particular person or company. However, such addresses are often spoofed, or altered to appear to come from machines that may be half a world away from the suspect's true location.

> "The Internet is the first thing that humanity has built that humanity doesn't understand, the largest experiment in anarchy that we have ever had."[14]
>
> —Eric Schmidt, executive chair of Alphabet.

Then, assuming authorities can identify one or more suspects, it may not be easy to bring them to trial. Many cybercrimes target US interests from abroad, possibly from countries that have weak or no laws against offenses involving computers. Furthermore, there are few international agreements that cover cybercrime.

Some countries may tolerate cybercrime as long as it is not directed at domestic interests. For example, some countries might tolerate industrial espionage that benefits their own companies at the expense of American competitors.

Extradition (bringing defendants to the United States to face trial) can thus take years, if it is possible at all. Extradition can only be done by meeting the detailed requirements spelled out in a treaty between the nations involved. This can include demonstrating that one has evidence of a specific crime and giving assurances that the accused person's legal rights will be protected. An example of this lengthy process comes from 2009, when the US government indicted several hackers (mainly Russians) who were part of a cybercrime ring. One alleged ringleader, Vladimir Drinkman, was arrested in the Netherlands in June 2012 but did not face trial in the United States until April 2015, following a protracted legal struggle.

Vladimir Drinkman, a hacker who was indicted for his alleged role in a cybercrime ring, is escorted to a Netherlands court proceeding shortly before his extradition to the United States in 2015. The process of identifying, catching, and trying hackers can be lengthy.

Prosecuting Cybercrime

Before going to trial, prosecutors must also determine the appropriate criminal charges. The main federal law governing cybercrime that involves computer intrusions, unauthorized retrieval of data, or damage to computer systems is the Computer Fraud and Abuse Act of 1986. Besides criminal prosecution, the law allows victims to sue perpetrators for damages. While the original version of the law makes it possible to prosecute the digital equivalents of trespassing, burglary, or vandalism, it is not always easy to apply the law to the more esoteric activities of cybercriminals, such as selling information about security flaws or using stolen information for extortion or blackmail.

However, later amendments—such as the 2008 Theft Enforcement and Restitution Act—gave the law a broader reach, including making it illegal to threaten to steal data, threaten to disclose sensitive data (as with blackmail), or prevent access to data (as with ransomware). Early in 2015 Barack Obama proposed several other legislative measures that would cover additional computer offenses. For example, the sale of certain kinds of malware, including spyware, would be made illegal. It would also be illegal to set up or sell access to botnets. The proposed legislation would also allow authorities to prosecute anyone who possesses or traffics in stolen data, no matter what country they are in, as long as the information originated from a US bank. This provision is intended to address the fact that currently, it is difficult to prosecute crimes that involve the global black market in financial information because data and money move freely and often end up in foreign countries.

Another proposed provision would strengthen the ability to prosecute insiders—people who work in government or at private companies who have legitimate access to information (such as online accounts) but obtain it for illegitimate purposes—such as selling it on the criminal black market. However, while such legal reforms would help fight cybercrime, a balance must be struck between achieving security and overzealously prosecuting harmless activities. For example, David M. Bitkower of the US Department of

Justice noted in a Senate hearing that such a law could be used to prosecute individuals who technically misused the Internet but not toward a criminal end. "The statute could be construed to permit prosecution of a person who accesses the internet to check baseball scores at lunchtime in violation of her employer's strict internet use policy," Bitkower noted. "Or someone who accesses a dating website but lies about his height even though the site's terms of service require users to provide only accurate information."[16] The proposed law would try to guard against this by requiring situations to meet one of the following conditions: (1) any information accessed must be worth $5,000 or more, (2) the access must be in furtherance of a separate felony offense, or (3) the information must be stored on a computer used by or on behalf of a government agency.

As of mid-2016, however, Congress had not acted on these proposals. They continue to be vigorously debated, with advocates of online user rights such as the Electronic Frontier Foundation generally opposing the changes.

Changing Corporate Attitudes

Fighting cybercrime effectively requires a great deal of cooperation, both between companies in a particular industry and between private business and government agencies. However, companies can be reluctant to involve the government in investigating cyberattacks. Probing the details of the attack might reveal lax security or regulatory violations, which could result in fines or lawsuits for the company. Also, any additional publicity about an attack is typically unwelcome, because it could cause customers to lose confidence in a company (following the Target breach in November 2013, for example, the retailer's sales dropped 5.3 percent compared to the previous year). Stock prices, too, could drop.

To push for more disclosure, some states have passed laws that require companies to report any breaches that compromise customer data. Such laws seem to be effective at bringing at least some attacks out of the woodwork. When such a law took effect

Public Health in Cyberspace

Both physical viruses and the computer viruses used by hackers spread by finding vulnerable targets. For both kinds of infections, waiting until the virus has spread may mean it is too late to prevent a full-blown epidemic. Thus, prevention is emphasized. People are urged to be vaccinated against the flu, wash their hands, and handle food carefully. The computer equivalent to vaccination is using properly updated antivirus and firewall programs. The equivalent to washing hands and being careful with food is being wary of suspicious e-mail, social network posts, and attachments.

Despite such measures, malware outbreaks will occur. In public health, the Centers for Disease Control and Protection (CDC) is in charge of detecting and responding to epidemic threats. A 2011 report prepared for the US Department of Homeland Security suggests that cybersecurity agencies could learn valuable lessons from how the CDC operates: "The cyber version of the CDC would . . . serve as a hub for cooperation with all the various other state and international agencies as well as nonstate actors that matter in cyberspace, just as the CDC works collectively with groups like the World Health Organization (WHO) all the way down to local hospitals, universities, and research centers." The report also suggests that one major job of a "cyber CDC" would be to "'drain the Internet swamp' of botnets through efforts to take infected computers offline."

P.W. Singer and Allan Friedman, *Cybersecurity and Cyberwar: What Everyone Needs to Know.* New York: Oxford University Press, 2014, pp. 174–75.

in California in 2005, for example, fifty-one companies reported breaches, compared to just three reports filed the year before.

Consumers might also be able to put pressure on companies to improve security by patronizing only those businesses that seem committed to protecting their information. "When you go

into a restaurant, you get a health rating, at least in California, from the health inspector," says Kevin Haley, director of security response at Symantec. "We don't have anything like that in terms of security. Maybe that's something that we need. It would certainly cause companies to start doing the right thing."[17]

Ray Rothrock, CEO and chair of security firm RedSeal, suggests the government could reward companies with good security practices by protecting them from some of the financial and legal consequences of an attack. Businesses might undergo an evaluation of how securely their computers and networks are set up. Companies that scored high enough in the review and agreed to report any breaches would receive legal protection, a so-called safe harbor. Says Rothrock, "Sooner or later, businesses will recognize it's in everyone's best interest . . . to admit and accept their security vulnerabilities—in a reliable, trustworthy and transparent environment where businesses can evaluate vulnerabilities, implement protections and monitor incidents on an ongoing basis."[18]

The Encryption Dilemma

One of the most effective tools for protecting information from attack—encryption—can also pose an obstacle to investigating crime or terrorism. Every day, people depend on encryption to keep them safe when they shop, bank, or otherwise live their lives online. Major companies such as Google, Microsoft, and Apple all routinely provide automatic encryption for e-mail and other data stored on devices.

However, law enforcement agencies such as the FBI and even local police officials want—and many would argue, need—a way to decrypt the contents of a computer or mobile device that has been seized from a suspect after a crime has been committed. This issue came to widespread attention in 2016 when the FBI sought to compel Apple to provide access to an iPhone that had belonged to Syed Rizwan Farook, who on December 2, 2015, killed fourteen people and injured twenty-two in a mass shooting in San Bernardino, California. Apple, however, had designed the system so that only users have their phone's access code (similar to a PIN number). Furthermore, if more than ten attempts are made to guess the code, the device automatically erases its data.

> "When you go into a restaurant, you get a health rating. . . . We don't have anything like that in terms of security. Maybe that's something that we need."[17]
>
> —Kevin Haley, director of security response at Symantec.

The FBI filed for a court order that would have required Apple to create and install a version of its operating system that could bypass the restrictions. This would allow the FBI to run a program that could repeatedly try access codes until the device was opened and the decrypted data could be seen. Apple strongly opposed granting the order, arguing that if it were forced to create a back door that could bypass the device's security, such software would inevitably spread (or be re-created), which would in turn threaten the security of all iPhone users. Other companies such as Amazon, Google, and Microsoft supported Apple's position, as did many leading technologists, the Electronic Frontier Foundation, and the American Civil Liberties Union.

Just as the judge was preparing to conduct a hearing on the matter, the FBI abruptly withdrew its request. It turned out that the FBI had hired an unidentified group of hackers to find a way to break into the iPhone, reportedly paying more than $1.3 million for their successful effort. This development in turn aroused considerable concern. The Edward Snowden revelations had already suggested that the NSA had exploited numerous software flaws to intercept communications without telling the companies involved. The idea of the government itself becoming a hacker and potentially weakening security, even for the good cause of fighting crime and terrorism, is troubling to many.

Protesters call on the FBI to halt its efforts to force Apple to provide access to encrypted data on the iPhone that belonged to the man who carried out the 2015 mass shooting in San Bernardino, California. Encryption adds a layer of protection for consumers but also poses an obstacle in criminal investigations.

In 2016 Senators Dianne Feinstein and Richard Burr introduced a bill, the Compliance with Court Orders Act, that would require communications companies to provide unencrypted versions of encrypted user information when ordered by a court or help the government unencrypt it. The bill would not prevent companies from providing encryption, but it would require companies to be able to defeat their own encryption in order to be able to make the information available.

The bill aroused immediate opposition. Kevin Bankston, director of New America's Open Technology Institute, warned that by forcing companies to provide facilities for breaking their own encryption, the bill would lead companies to abandon encryption—or at best to provide only weakened encryption. He said that the law in effect

> instructs every tech vendor in America to use either backdoored encryption or no encryption at all, even though practically every security expert in the country would tell you that means laying down our arms in the constant fight to secure our data against thieves, hackers, and spies. This bill would not only be surrendering America's cybersecurity but also its tech economy, as foreign competitors would continue to offer—and bad guys would still be able to easily use!—more secure products and services.[19]

The bill soon stalled, having failed to find support in the White House or among enough other senators. However, even if bills compelling companies to in effect hack their own data protections are defeated, the need to strike a balance between having access to communications from criminals or terrorists and providing online security for everyone else remains.

International Cooperation to Address a Global Problem

As has been proved over and over, cybercrime transcends national boundaries. Currently, there are few international laws or treaties that effectively help nations cooperate to fight cybercrime. This is

Responding to a Cyber Attack

In 2014 even the isolated and impoverished dictatorship of North Korea showed it could launch a major cyberattack. Sony Pictures was preparing to release *The Interview*, a comedy starring Seth Rogen and James Franco that was about a plot to assassinate North Korean leader Kim Jong-un. Jong-un was apparently offended by the storyline. Attackers believed to be working for the North Korean government stole confidential data from Sony's computers, including Social Security numbers and other personal details, causing about $100 million in damage. At first, Sony canceled the film's release because of the threat of further attacks. But after it was criticized for bowing to threats, the company made a limited release of the film.

Meanwhile, Barack Obama and his top advisers were deciding how the government should respond to the attack. One adviser, NSA director Admiral Michael S. Rogers, argued that a strong response was necessary: "The whole world is watching how we as a nation respond," he said. "And if we don't acknowledge this, if we don't name names here, it will only . . . encourage others to decide . . . 'this [attack] must be something [the United States is] comfortable [with] and willing to accept.'" Rogers's argument was accepted, largely because North Korea's actions were viewed as a blatant attempt to suppress free speech. The US government publicly named North Korea as the attacker and condemned the attack. Later, the United States also imposed economic sanctions against some key North Korean individuals.

Quoted in Ellen Nakashima, "Why the Sony Hack Drew an Unprecedented U.S. Response Against North Korea," *Washington Post*, January 15, 2015. www.washingtonpost.com.

in part because addressing any issue (such as global warming, for example) through international action is a slow, complicated process. Countries have to both become aware of how significant a problem online security is for the global economy and become convinced that addressing it is in their national interest. Currently, with hackers around the world attacking institutions in other countries and data being sold on underground markets, the situation is chaotic. "Today's cyber world is akin to medieval Europe,"[20] notes David Tohn, a military officer and national security expert. Tohn hopes that governments and private companies alike might come to see how cooperating to secure the online world would be in everyone's best interests.

Cybersecurity is already a major issue in many international negotiations, including treaties dealing with trade, intellectual property, and cooperation in law enforcement. As the impact of cybercrime continues to grow, there will be more pressure on corporations, national governments, and international agencies to find more effective ways to combat it.

> "Today's cyber world is akin to medieval Europe."[20]
>
> —David Tohn, national security expert.

CHAPTER FIVE

The Future of Online Security

O nline security is a tough, multifaceted problem that poses many difficulties, and new concerns are constantly emerging. For example, the basic services people rely on for survival increasingly depend on complicated and potentially vulnerable computer networks. Furthermore, the fact that even the most ordinary devices are increasingly becoming Internet enabled—in what has been dubbed the Internet of Things (IoT)—means that a successful hack on one device can end up compromising many others.

The future offers many exciting new products—intelligent assistants, helpful robots, self-driving cars, and smart houses, for example. However, all these developments increase what security professionals call the attack surface—the number of potential areas in which vulnerabilities can be found and exploited.

Should We Trust Artificial Intelligence?

Today a number of apps such as Apple's Siri or Google Now are available, and they are particularly useful on mobile devices. These apps respond to spoken questions or requests. For example, iPhone users can not only ask Siri to remind them to get milk, they can have Siri recognize when they are in the grocery store and remind them then. A user can also have Siri make or reschedule appointments, much like a personal secretary or executive assistant. Siri can link to a variety of other applications to carry out tasks, such as connecting to OpenTable to make a reservation at one's favorite restaurant. These apps are made possible by advances in artificial intelligence, including the ability to understand ordinary human language, "learn" about people's preferences, and use that knowledge to respond to later requests.

However, to carry out these tasks, an intelligent assistant must "know" a lot about a person's family, coworkers, friends, location, and daily activities. For example, if someone asks Siri to "call Mom," the app not only has to have her contact information but also categorize her as that family member. To be able to remind a user to buy milk while in the grocery store, the software needs the phone's GPS to keep track of the user's location. Current intelligent assistants and more advanced ones still in development can know what restaurants users prefer, what kind of food they like, and when a user typically has lunch. Potentially, that is a lot of detailed information—and the question becomes who has (or should have) access to it.

Self-driving cars (pictured) and smart houses represent a new and exciting Internet-connected technological future. They also expand vulnerabilities that can be exploited by unscrupulous individuals and entities.

Many users are already concerned about how information about their web searches and other online activities is being stored by businesses. With apps such as Siri, however, information is potentially being acquired even when the user has not gone online to connect to a particular service. For example, Apple has revealed that it digitally records everything said to Siri and stores it for up to two years (although after six months the data is no longer associated with a specific user). These recordings are sent by Apple to other companies that review it to try to improve Siri's performance. How well that data is protected from possible intruders, however, becomes an issue. Another issue lies in the fact that in order for the user to say "Hey, Siri" to get the app's attention, the phone's microphone must be on all the time. This raises the possibility that hackers may be able to tap into everything the phone "hears," not just requests to Siri.

As more such apps and intelligent assistants become increasingly useful and widespread, people are likely to increasingly depend on them to keep track of their daily activities. Meanwhile, the data that is collected could amount to a detailed profile of the user's contacts, locations visited, daily routine, and even personal habits. If an app has poor security and can be hacked, accessing such profiles could provide many opportunities for criminals.

In the old days, enterprising rings of burglars would sometimes cultivate friendships with butlers or maids in order to learn, for example, when a wealthy family was likely to be away so the house could be plundered. Today information stored by apps such as the recent purchase of an expensive TV or the family's airline ticket purchases and other vacation plans could provide similar opportunities.

Risky Robots?

Another area where artificial intelligence brings new capabilities but also new risks is robotics. One often thinks of robots as they appear in the movies—friendly or menacing, but humanlike. However, the real robots that increasingly surround us may be less obviously robotic. They are devices that carry out various tasks

Checking Out Security

In some stores payments can now be made using smartphone apps such as Apple Pay or Android Pay. This can be convenient—there is no wallet full of cards to keep track of, and no swiping is needed. However, if the phone has to connect to the Internet to complete the transaction, delays caused by slow connections could lead to longer lines and frustrated customers.

Alternatively, preapproved virtual cards can be generated on the phone ahead of time, so no online connection is necessary. However, this information could be stolen by hackers using malware, then copied to another phone and used to make purchases. To guard against this, a unique profile could be used to identify a particular phone using location data (based on GPS coordinates or nearby Wi-Fi hotspots) together with a list of the number and type of apps installed on the device. Someone who has the stolen data but does not have the same phone would therefore not be able to complete transactions.

Observing the evolution of payment systems and security features, security researcher Richard Moulos says that "in this era of increasingly clever cybercriminals, every Internet-connected activity creates its own security issues. . . . [However,] in an ironic twist, one of the devices that has caused security concerns—smartphones—can serve the goal of security by helping authenticate users."

Richard Moulos, "Why Mobile Payments Adoption Has Been Slow—and Why That's About to Change," *Wired*, January 2015. www.wired.com.

with minimal or no supervision. They range from little Roombas and other robot vacuum cleaners all the way up to appliances. In many ways even today's cars are like robots, and they are becoming more so every day.

These complex, highly automated devices are often online—they are connected to other nearby devices, Wi-Fi or cellular networks, or even to the Internet. This connectivity makes them convenient but also vulnerable to being tampered with by hackers. A dramatic demonstration of this vulnerability came in a 2015 test in which security researchers showed how they could use a laptop and cell phone to take control of a Jeep Cherokee while *Wired* reporter Andy Greenberg was driving. As Greenberg reported, "They disabled my brakes, honked the horn, jerked the seat belt, and commandeered the steering wheel."[21] In another test, the researchers proceeded to send the car (safely) into a ditch.

> "They disabled my brakes, honked the horn, jerked the seat belt, and commandeered the steering wheel."[21]
>
> —*Wired* reporter Andy Greenberg.

This hacking was possible because the Cherokee, like most modern cars, has an internal network containing more computers than the average home—not to mention Wi-Fi and cellular connections. By exploiting a flaw, the hackers were able to send commands to the devices within the car, such as its engines, wheels, steering system, and brakes. After being informed of the vulnerability in its car, automaker Chrysler quickly updated the Cherokee's software. However, while physically taking over and controlling a car is not easy and would require detailed knowledge of the systems on different models of vehicles, the test demonstrated the scary possibility that one's smart car could be hijacked. The result might be a ransomware demand for payment to regain control of one's car.

Fully autonomous, self-driving cars may be available to consumers early in the 2020s. While such vehicles are expected to reduce traffic fatalities caused by human error or drunk driving, they could introduce new problems. The type of driverless car favored by Google, for example, would have no steering wheel, brake, or other driver controls. If such a car were electronically hijacked, the "driver" (in reality, more like a helpless passenger) could be driven to a remote location and robbed or even kidnapped. Alternatively, if built-in safeguards (such as collision detection or lane keeping) could be bypassed, the car, with occupants locked inside, could be driven into a wall or over an embankment.

Overall, self-driving cars promise to be safer, more efficient, and accessible to more people than human-driven ones. However, manufacturers and regulators will have to include robust security and safety systems if this new technology is to be widely adopted—and trusted.

The Internet of (Hackable) Things

Cars are not the only things getting smarter. Designers of devices of all sorts, from thermostats to lights to refrigerators, are trying to find ways to equip them to respond to their environment, their users, and even each other. Such devices, already available or on the drawing board, include heating and air-conditioning systems that sense the presence of people and adjust settings for comfort, refrigerators that can order groceries, and stoves that can start preparing dinner in response to a text message.

A model demonstrates the connective features of a smart refrigerator. Smart appliances and other household devices will require more sophisticated security and safety systems to thwart hackers.

Such connections may be just the beginning of transforming how our technological environment works. According to Peter Middleton, research director at the Gartner research firm:

> By 2020, connectivity will be a standard feature, even for processors costing less than $1. This opens up the possibility of connecting just about anything, from the very simple to the very complex, to offer remote control, monitoring and sensing. As product designers dream up ways to exploit the inherent connectivity that will be offered in intelligent products, we expect the variety of devices offered to explode.[22]

A 2015 report by Cisco and DHL estimates that the number of connected devices in the IoT will grow from 15 billion to 50 billion by 2020. Meanwhile, the economic impact in terms of new products and new forms of utilization of existing resources could be $8 trillion by 2025. However, this will multiply the number of potential security problems, according to Mark Bower, global product manager for data security at HPE Security. "Over the next 10 years, the Internet of Things will create yet more opportunities for attackers to create new revenue streams that have previously not been available," warns Bower. "This quickly becomes about personal security of an individual or even a whole country."[23]

Essentially, the IoT extends the Internet throughout the physical world, which allows apps to enable users to control lighting, heating, air-conditioning, appliances, and much more. However, in the rush to add new features, adequate protection against intruders coming into the network is often not provided. As veteran computer security researchers Peter J. and Dorothy E. Denning note, "The burgeoning Internet of Things is widely regarded as a potential security disaster because designers of individual things often pare down their operating system to bare essentials, such as wireless connections, and do not preserve security technologies. These devices contain many more vulnerabilities than do [regular] commercial operating systems."[24]

What Anyone Can Do

Security has two components: safe practices and constant awareness. Here are some steps that anyone can take to be safer in the digital world and to help make cybercrime less attractive.

- Use strong passwords, mixing letters, numbers, and special characters.
- Do not use the same password for multiple sites.
- Consider using a password manager program to generate unique, strong passwords.
- Choose security questions for which it is unlikely people can find answers online.
- Use multifactor authentication for sensitive sites such as bank and e-mail accounts. This is similar to using PINs on bank cards. Typically, a code is sent to a user's phone to help verify his or her identity.
- Set operating systems and software such as web browsers to automatically keep up-to-date with security patches.
- Use up-to-date wireless security and a strong router password.
- Keep regular backups both in the cloud and on a separate drive that is disconnected when not in use.
- Download mobile apps only from authorized app stores. Keep devices' operating systems and apps up-to-date.
- Read the privacy policy for each app or service. Note what information is collected and what can be done with it. If available, choose settings that maximize privacy.

If the proper security measures are not provided, then the connectivity offers attackers new ways into the network of a home or other building. For example, if a smart refrigerator is part of a home network and is also connected to the Internet (enabling it to order groceries from Amazon, perhaps), an intruder could scan the network to find the device's address. The intruder could guess its password (which might even still be set to the factory default), connect to the home's central router, and possibly take over the whole network. As a result, alarm systems could be disabled. Surveillance cameras could be turned on their users, enabling intruders to know what (and who) is in the home.

It can be difficult to recognize such potential vulnerabilities because neither designers nor consumers are used to thinking about a world in which everything is smart and everything is connected. According to Corey Nachreiner, chief technology officer at WatchGuard Technologies, failing to conceive of devices as computers poses a huge risk, "in part because most people don't think, 'computer' when they look at certain IoT devices. Unfortunately, the result is that people also don't associate the same risk with these devices as they do with computers. Even though the risk profile is much the same."[25]

A New Kind of War

While people struggle to anticipate the possible vulnerabilities of their new devices and connections, the basic systems they have long depended on for daily survival have also come under the threat of potentially devastating online attacks. Indeed, in recent years cyberattacks have begun to directly target infrastructure—vital physical systems such as power plants, water systems, or transportation.

This threat was first brought to public attention by an incident in Iran in 2010, at a nuclear facility at Natanz. The facility was protected by modern radar and air defense systems, making it difficult to destroy by conventional means. However, it was crippled by the stealthy logic of computer code—a complicated program called Stuxnet. Stuxnet worked by probing four previously unknown flaws in the Windows operating system that ran the software controlling centrifuges used to enrich uranium. (This state-of-the art digital weapon may have been physically brought into the closely guarded facility on a USB thumb drive by an unsuspecting employee.) Once it spread through the systems, Stuxnet created fake data that made it look to the operators like everything was operating normally, even as it sent commands to the centrifuges that made them speed up and down repeatedly until, apparently, vibrations destroyed the machines.

While it was unclear exactly who was responsible for the cyberattack (though the United States and Israel were the chief suspects), one thing was certain: cyberweapons could not only destroy information, but also physical systems—and just as thoroughly as a missile or bomb. This point was demonstrated again in August 2012 when Aramco, a major oil company in Saudi Arabia (an ally of the United States), was attacked by a virus that effectively destroyed thirty thousand of its computers. Iran's own sophisticated hacker teams were believed to be responsible for this work, likely as retaliation for the Stuxnet attack.

Governments and militaries around the world took notice of these cyberspace battles. "Of late, an Internet tornado has swept across the world," noted a report by the Chinese Academy of Military Sciences. "Every nation and military can't be passive but is making preparations to fight the Internet war."[26] US military and intelligence officials warned that the nation was not prepared for cyberattacks by foreign governments. "If the nation went to war today, in a cyberwar, we would lose," Mike McConnell, former director of national intelligence, told a US Senate committee. "We're the most vulnerable. We're the most connected. We have the most to lose."[27]

> "If the nation went to war today, in a cyberwar, we would lose. We're the most vulnerable. We're the most connected. We have the most to lose."[27]
>
> —Mike McConnell, US director of national intelligence from 2007 to 2009.

One of the many difficulties in addressing this problem is the fact that it would be very hard to identify cyberwar attackers. Unlike a missile, whose origin and path can be tracked by satellite or radar, the "launching pad" for a cyberattack can be well hidden within a series of obscured Internet addresses and possibly servers in uninvolved countries. With such uncertainty surrounding the attacker's identity, it would be difficult to make accusations or decide how to retaliate.

Cyberterrorists and Vulnerable Infrastructure

Cyberattacks conducted by terrorist groups may pose an even trickier problem. Terrorists have long used the Internet and a variety of communications and social networking apps to recruit members and teach them how to make bombs, poison gas, and other weapons. For example, Dzhohkhar Tsarnaev, who along with his brother Tamerlan bombed the Boston Marathon in 2013, admitted to police that the pair had learned how to build a pressure-cooker bomb from an article in al Qaeda's online magazine, *Inspire*. Terrorists also team up with regular cybercriminals in an alliance of convenience, learning to hack into bank accounts or use stolen credit cards to help fund operations such as the 2004 Madrid bombings (which killed 190 people and wounded 2000 more) or the bombings that killed 52 and injured more than 700 in London in 2007, both of which were financed in this way. A growing fear, however, is that terrorists could use cyberweapons similar to Stuxnet to directly damage or disrupt the physical systems on which modern societies depend.

Power systems—electrical, hydro, and nuclear—are among the more critical and vulnerable targets. To protect them, the federal government has been working with manufacturers to make software and hardware changes that would make it more difficult for intruders to compromise the control systems that run such power plants. However, this process is difficult and time-consuming because the control systems themselves are made by a number of manufacturers, and new features are always being added.

Another potential target is the system of pumps, treatment plants, and pipelines that deliver clean, safe water. Some of these systems have already been attacked—for example, in 2016 hackers exploited a poorly secured web server (whose location was kept confidential for security reasons) to access a water system. They were able to take over the plant's valves and flow control systems. They then increased the amount of water-treatment chemicals flowing into the system. Fortunately, operators were automatically alerted and soon reversed the changes. Transportation is another vulnerable area. In 2012 Secretary of Defense

Government and business are working together to make it more difficult for terrorists to attack electrical power systems, water treatment plants, and other infrastructure. These are considered vulnerable targets for cyberattacks.

Leon Panetta warned that "an aggressor nation or extremist group could gain control of critical switches and derail passenger trains, or trains loaded with lethal chemicals," resulting in a "cyber Pearl Harbor."[28]

Privacy advocates have argued that some of these threats may be overblown. Nevertheless, there is good evidence that hackers and possibly terrorists are probing systems, perhaps in an effort to figure out how to attack them in the future. According to the 2015 Dell Security Annual Threat Report, attacks on supervisory control and data acquisition systems rose from 91,676 in 2013 to 163,228 in 2014. The actual number may be even higher, as many attacks are not reported because most regulations only require attacks to be reported if they involve personal or financial information.

The consequences of a major infrastructure attack could be enormous. What would happen if a well-coordinated attack overloaded the tightly balanced electrical grid and knocked out power to an entire region of the United States? Economist and government security analyst Scott Borg believes that such an event would be "equivalent to 40 to 50 large hurricanes striking all at once. It's greater economic damage than any modern economy ever suffered. . . . It's greater than the Great Depression. It's greater than the damage we did with strategic bombing on Germany in World War II."[29]

How does one assess the risks and make an appropriate effort to minimize them? On the one hand, considerable attention is being paid to the security of power and water systems. The fact that there has not yet been a successful attack on such high-value targets may indicate that it would be difficult for a terrorist group or enemy government to actually bring down a large power grid. However, many argue that the mere thought of one taking place is reason enough to protect such systems with strong layers of security.

Becoming an Informed Cybercitizen

The threat to infrastructure, along with the IoT and the continuing emergence of new kinds of devices and applications, will ensure that online security remains a complex challenge, like a puzzle with many pieces. Indeed, with governments, technologists, businesses, and consumers scrambling just to catch up to yesterday's threats, it may seem that there is not much more that ordinary people can do—but that is not true.

When it comes to the skills and perspectives needed to stay safe online, there is an education gap that must be bridged. Doing so begins with the need to make sure that middle and high school students receive systematic education in how to safely navigate the world of the web, social media, and mobile apps. Today this is as essential as traditional classes on subjects such as health, home economics, or drivers' education.

Students who go on to prepare for careers in information technology will need additional education in security. A study by the security firm CloudPassage found that only one of the top thirty-six college computer science programs in the United States required that students take a cybersecurity course in order to graduate. CloudPassage CEO Robert Thomas notes that "with more than 200,000 open cybersecurity jobs in 2015 in the U.S. alone, and the number of threat surfaces exponentially increasing, there's a growing skills gap between the bad actors and the good guys."[30]

More broadly, computer users need to be proactive and alert all the time. Consumers need to choose apps and services carefully, balancing the value of new features with implications for privacy and security. Consumers and businesses alike need to engage with legislators and agencies to promote regulations and policies that are based on both a realistic understanding of technology and human behavior. At the same time, a careful balance must be found between protecting society from threats and promoting individual privacy and liberty.

> "There's a growing skills gap between the bad actors and the good guys."[30]
>
> —Robert Thomas, CEO of CloudPassage.

SOURCE NOTES

Introduction: Meeting a Growing Threat

1. Quoted in White House, "Remarks by the President on Securing Our Nation's Cyber Infrastructure," press release, May 29, 2009. www.whitehouse.gov.
2. Quoted in Wendy St. Clair, "Cyber Security in 2016: Reflecting on the World Economic Forum," *Forbes*, February 4, 2016. www.forbes.com.

Chapter One: Threats to Online Security

3. Ben Hammersley, "Check Against Delivery," September 11, 2007. http://files.neilgaiman.com.
4. Quoted in Willie Sutton and Edward Linn, *Where the Money Was: The Memoirs of a Bank Robber.* Viking, 1976, p. 160.
5. Quoted in P.W. Singer and Allan Friedman, *Cybersecurity and Cyberwar: What Everyone Needs to Know.* New York: Oxford University Press, 2014. pp. 88–89.
6. Quoted in *Weekend Edition Sunday*, "3 Voices, 1 Threat: Personal Stories of Cyberhacking," NPR, January 25, 2015. www.npr.org.
7. Jonathan M. Gitlin, "OPM Got Hacked and All I Got Was This Stupid E-Mail," Ars Technica, July 11, 2015. http://arstechnica.com.
8. Quoted in John Seabrook, "Network Insecurity: Are We Losing the Battle Against Cyber Crime?," *New Yorker*, May 20, 2013. www.newyorker.com.

Chapter Two: The Problem with Being Connected

9. Mat Honan, "How Apple and Amazon Security Flaws Led to My Epic Hacking," *Wired*, August 6, 2012. www.wired.com.
10. Quoted in *OnlyMyEmail* (blog), "Wells Fargo Bank Security Alert Phishing Example," 2016. http://blog.onlymyemail.com.

Chapter Three: Building a Safer Cyberspace

11. Quoted in World Economic Forum and McKinsey & Company, "Risk and Responsibility in a Hyperconnected World," 2014. http://reports.weforum.org.
12. Brian Krebs, "Krebs on Security," 2013. http://krebsonsecurity.com.
13. Singer and Friedman, *Cybersecurity and Cyberwar*, p. 36.

Chapter Four: Regulating and Policing the Digital Realm

14. Eric Schmidt and Jared Cohen, *The New Digital Age: Transforming Nations, Businesses, and Our Lives*. New York: Vintage, 2014, p. 285.
15. John Perry Barlow, "A Declaration of the Independence of Cyberspace," Electronic Frontier Foundation, February 8, 1996. www.eff.org.
16. Statement of David M. Bitkower before the Subcommittee on Crime and Terrorism, Committee on the Judiciary, US Senate, at a Hearing Entitled "Cyber Crime: Modernizing Our Legal Framework for the Informatiion Age," July 8, 2015. www.judiciary.senate.gov.
17. Quoted in Anita Balakrishnan, "The Hospital Held Hostage by Hackers," CNBC, February 16, 2016. www.cnbc.com.
18. Ray Rothrock, "Our Cybersecurity Problem Is a Lack of Working Safe Harbor Rules," *Forbes*, December 21, 2015. www.forbes.com.
19. Quoted in John Eggerton, "Draft Bill Would Compel Decryption by Communications Companies," Broadcasting & Cable, April 8, 2016. www.broadcastingcable.com.
20. David Tohn, "Digital Trench Warfare," *Boston Globe*, June 11, 2009. http://archive.boston.com.

Chapter Five: The Future of Online Security

21. Andy Greenberg, "Hackers Remotely Kill a Jeep on the Highway—with Me in It," *Wired*, July 21, 2015. www.wired.com.
22. Quoted in Preeti Guar, "Impact of the Internet of Things," *PCQuest*, October 2014. www.pcquest.com.
23. Quoted in Kathryn Cave, "How Will Tech Have Transformed Our Lives by 2026?," IDG Connect, April 21, 2016. www.idgconnect.com.
24. Peter J. Denning and Dorothy E. Denning, "Cybersecurity Is Harder than Building Bridges," *American Scientist*, May/June 2016, p. 154.
25. Quoted in Cave, "How Will Tech Have Transformed Our Lives by 2026?"
26. Quoted in Singer and Friedman, *Cybersecurity and Cyberwar*, p. 7.
27. Quoted in Mark Clayton, "The New Cyber Arms Race," *Christian Science Monitor*, March 7, 2011. www.csmonitor.com.
28. Quoted in Seabrook, "Network Insecurity."
29. Quoted in Jean Meserve, "Staged Cyber Attack Reveals Vulnerability in Power Grid," CNN, September 26, 2007. www.cnn.com.
30. Quoted in *Security*, "U.S. Universities Failing in Cybersecurity Education," April 14, 2016. www.securitymagazine.com.

American Civil Liberties Union (ACLU)
125 Broad St., 18th Floor
New York, NY 10004
phone: (212) 549-2500
website: www.aclu.org

As part of its general advocacy and litigation for civil liberties, the ACLU becomes involved in issues involving privacy, liberty, and legal process in cyberspace.

Center for Strategic and International Studies
1800 K St. NW
Washington, DC 20006
phone: (202) 887-0200
website: www.csis.org

The Center for Strategic and International Studies is a think tank that conducts analyses and policy studies involving political, economic, and security issues worldwide, including cyberwar and cyberterrorism.

Computer Emergency Readiness Team
Department of Homeland Security
245 Murray Lane SW, Bldg. 410
Washington, DC 20598
phone: (703) 235-5110
website: www.us-cert.gov

A division of the Department of Homeland Security, the Computer Emergency Readiness Team is charged with detecting and responding to cyberattacks that threaten the government or infrastructure of the United States.

Electronic Frontier Foundation (EFF)
815 Eddy St.
San Francisco, CA 94109
phone: (415) 436-9333
website: www.eff.org

The EFF advocates and litigates for civil liberties and privacy in cyberspace and provides regular updates on current developments and issues.

Federal Bureau of Investigation (FBI)

935 Pennsylvania Ave. NW
Washington, DC 20535
phone: (202) 324-3000

The FBI is a federal law enforcement agency that investigates cyber-crime and cyberterrorism and offers resources on a variety of related subjects.

Internet Society

1775 Wiehle Ave., Suite 201
Reston VA 20190
phone: (703) 439-2120
website: www.internetsociety.org

The Internet Society develops and promotes policies relating to the governance of the Internet and the development of its technology.

Pew Research Center

1615 L St. NW, Suite 800
Washington, DC 20036
phone: (202) 419-4300
website: www.pewinternet.org

The Pew Research Center conducts surveys and offers analyses of issues and trends relating to the use of the Internet and other aspects of digital life.

Ponemon Institute

2308 US 31 N.
Traverse City, MI 49686
phone: (800) 887-3118
website: www.ponemon.org

The Ponemon Institute conducts research on privacy, data protection, and information security policy.

Books

Matthew Bailey, *Complete Guide to Internet Privacy, Anonymity & Security.* Nerel Online, 2015.

Marc Goodman, *Future Crimes: Everything Is Connected, Everyone Is Vulnerable, and What We Can Do About It*. New York: Doubleday, 2015.

Thomas A. Johnson, *Cyber-Security: Protecting Critical Infrastructure from Cyber Attack and Cyber Warfare*. Boca Raton, FL: CRC, 2015.

Ted Koppel, *Lights Out: A Cyberattack, a Nation Unprepared, Surviving the Aftermath*. New York: Crown, 2015.

Kevin Mitnick, *Ghost in the Wires: My Adventures as the World's Most Wanted Hacker*. New York: Little, Brown, 2011.

P.W. Singer and Allan Friedman, *Cybersecurity and Cyberwar: What Everyone Needs to Know*. New York: Oxford University Press, 2014.

Internet Sources

Charles Doyle, "Cybercrime: A Sketch of 18 U.S.C. 1030 and Related Federal Criminal Laws," Congressional Research Service, October 15, 2014. www.fas.org/sgp/crs/misc/RS20830 .pdf.

James Fallows, "Hacked!," *Atlantic*, November 2011. www.the atlantic.com/magazine/archive/2011/11/hacked/308673.

Michael Kassner, "Photos: Top 10 Cybersecurity Issues to Watch in 2016," *TechRepublic*, November 30, 2015. www.tech republic.com/pictures/photos-top-10-cybersecurity-issues-to -watch-in-2016.

Lee Rainie and Shiva Maniam, "Americans Feel the Tensions Between Privacy and Security Concerns," Pew Research Center, February 19, 2016. www.pewresearch.org/fact-tank /2016/02/19/americans-feel-the-tensions-between-privacy -and-security-concerns.

Steve Ranger, "The New Art of War: How Trolls, Hackers and Spies Are Rewriting the Rules of Conflict," *TechRepublic*, Sep-

tember 15, 2015. www.techrepublic.com/article/the-new-art-of-war
-how-trolls-hackers-and-spies-are-rewriting-the-rules-of-conflict.

Reuters, "Exclusive: Fed Records Show Dozens of Cybersecurity Breaches," *New York Times*, June 1, 2016. www.nytimes.com/reuters /2016/06/01/technology/01reuters-usa-fed-cyber.html.

Michael Riley, "Missed Alarms and 40 Million Stolen Credit Card Numbers: How Target Blew It," Bloomberg, March 17, 2014. www.bloom berg.com/news/articles/2014-03-13/target-missed-warnings-in-epic -hack-of-credit-card-data.

Ken Roose, "Haunted by Hackers: A Suburban Family's Digital Ghost Story," *Fusion*, October 19, 2015. http://fusion.net/story/212802 /haunted-by-hackers-a-suburban-familys-digital-ghost-story.

John Searbrook, "Network Insecurity: Are We Losing the Battle Against Cyber Crime?," *New Yorker*, May 20, 2013. www.newyorker.com/mag azine/2013/05/20/network-insecurity.

Weekend Edition Sunday, "3 Voices, 1 Threat: Personal Stories of Cyberhacking," NPR, January 25, 2015. www.npr.org/2015/01/25 /379756181/3-voices-1-threat-personal-stories-of-cyberhacking.

Websites

Cybercrime, Federal Bureau of Investigation (www.fbi.gov). This site describes how the FBI investigates cybercrime, profiles recent cases, and offers resources to victims of attacks.

Cybercrime, Security Week (www.securityweek.com). Offers a variety of news and features about the activity of cybercriminals, legal cases, and security issues.

Cybersecurity News, *Security* (www.securitymagazine.com). Covers security news and issues, mainly from the point of view of how they affect businesses.

Cybersecurity, Tech News World (www.technewsworld.com). This site covers many of the latest developments involving security, surveillance, privacy, and related issues.

Online Privacy and Safety, Pew Research Center (www.pewre search.org). A regularly updated page listing publications by the Pew Research Center relating to privacy and security. The center's researchers regularly survey and analyze many aspects of the online world.

INDEX

PICTURE CREDITS